The Latch to the Garden

First published in 2018 by Dalzell Press.

Dalzell Press
54 Abbey Street
Bangor, N. Ireland
BT20 4JB

© Edmond Sheehy 2018

ISBN 978-0-9563864-5-8

The Latch to the Garden

Poetry from Edmond Sheehy

Dalzell Press

"Ach, die Gärten bist du" – Rilke

I and Thou

I want Jesus. I want Jesus today.
I want to see Jesus coming across the Brooklyn Bridge,
swinging his tools as he walks,
joking with other carpenters,
sun shining from behind him,
if he has to work he might as well enjoy himself.

I want to see Jesus in everyone I meet.
Every pedestrian has this divine majesty.
Every commuter is immutably perfect.
Every bicycle messenger is on a secret mission to save us.

I want to buy coffee from street vendor Jesus.
I want the World Trade Center Towers rebuilt
and I want it extra light with no sugar.

After I get to City Hall,
I want to shake the hand of Mayor Jesus.
I just hope that Jesus doesn't become
an Investment Banker after his term
and sell us municipal bonds endlessly.

I want to take the Six Train uptown.
to see Jesus, the conductor, the conveyor of Truth.
Over the rattling subway cars,
Jesus asks if I want to buy batteries.
Shy, immigrant Vietnamese Jesus,
he doesn't press his case.

When I get out at Astor Place,
I want to walk down St. Marks
and see in every tourist face Jesus.
Jesus is on horseback, policewoman Jesus,
she keeps us moving along.

On the old Tompkins Square bandshell,
I see Jesus guitar.
I hear the word made groove.
Everyone dancing in the park
abandons desires, distractions and doubts.
They only want to live for love,
happy for any chance
to help each other into paradise.

I am exhausted by the glory of Jesus.
Every blade of grass is ablaze on the lawn
The tenements echo with joy.

I seek respite in the shade
of the General Slocum fountain
beneath the trees upon the benches
where young mothers pin up their hair
to join the children bathed in grace.

So, I have come to know that the universe
is a conspiracy of mercy.
I close my eyes in peace.
and open them to see

the opportunities
to bring forth delight.

There is no love that is profane.
Here before us is the City of God.
Nothing is more holy.

Enjoy each other.
Multiply love by acts of kindness.
Glorify the streets of New York.
Sanctify every exchange.
Watch out for the bike messengers
and look both ways in traffic
for the love of Jesus.

Urbs canto

The flights of fire escapes
are strings in my lyre.
I would pluck across town
just to see you.

The avenues would be electric
with melody.
Traffic would swell and crescendo
in varied orchestrations
at each intersection
if you would just entertain
the notion
to see me.

At dawn, a triumphant man
would bellow aria
up the air shaft.
millions
would join us in chorus
from all the five boroughs.

Afterward, I would suggest
we go for a walk
so I could decode the evening
and what we had started.

Your words to me then
would be like an oboe solo
and all I have measured
would be explained.

The Gates

The gates of paradise are fire escapes,
they connect these alleyways to the stars.
In the dark no one can make out our shapes
as you kiss my temples then trace my scars.
I must confess when I caress your breast
in the yard behind your folks' apartment
that I feel happier than all the blessed;
your lips mean more than any sacrament.
We have no other home but this stone wall,
serenaded by choirs of the neighbors
cheering the TV as they watch baseball.
Exposed to heaven, in our place outdoors,
your face tonight outshines eternity,
focusing this city's ceaseless beauty.

A Jesuit at Hiroshima

"The explosion... is not a memory, it is a perpetual
experience...which does not pass with the ticking of the
clock." - Pedro Arrupe S.J. (survivor)

Surfaces radiated innate light.
The ordinary blazed struck with glory.
A roar erupted from a fearsome height
then scorched the air about the rectory.
I always strived to see God in all things.
Trees and offices leaning all one way,
patterns flash-set in skin where frayed cloth clings,
the flattened park where children used to play,
are proofs some say God is without mercy.
I cannot. Bloodied, after being thrown,
sifting through debris though I was weary,
where I heard moans I dug and tore at stone.
Trying to help, helped me stave off despair.
Love sustained me, love was all I could bear.

Confession

Recent snows about mountain laurel cling,
while from exposed cliff-face melt water flows.
Among bare briars, tufted tit mouse sing.
This early only blue-green lichen grows,
until trees will leaf and crowd out the light.
Spring teases but resists all advances.
Fields heave open that are frozen at night,
yet by day, mayflies dare to take chances.
Is it too soon now to confess to you?
My friends laugh when I say you are the one.
They poke fun, not knowing you as I do.
What reason have I for hesitation?
I behold such glory in your arms
as transcends this season's transient charms.

Clerics

They dress in black to vow their poverty,
the white collar's to mark obedience,
that ordained priests might serve with modesty
and remain restrained among innocents.
That office allowed men depraved with lust
close and constant access to school children,
to use authority to abuse trust
and destroy the faith of catechumen.
Those men wielding crozier betrayed us too
directing wolves into the flock, they prayed
none would notice, their sheep would keep in queue
and violated lambs would stay afraid.
abuse is dismissed if even discussed
while youthful trust lies trampled in the dust.

None are spared

Neither janitor nor banker is spared.
Innocents and villains all are vanquished.
Death takes its harvest whether we're prepared,
whatever we have wanted or we've wished.
When a soul is lifted from the body,
sins and good deeds are balanced in the scales,
measuring each life's worth without pity,
to judge in the end whether love prevails.
We are judges and executioners
and sentenced each moment we are alive.
We are asked to love our persecutors
to escape the jail we ourselves contrive.
Live for love and release eternity.
Live for less, be confined eternally.

Civics lesson

They will not hush the leaves upon the breeze.
I hear a rush of urges almost words
and I am lulled by ideologies
when trees are swarmed by migratory birds.
In cycles they come, I want to believe
their return marks the end of miseries,
that revolution will fix all I grieve,
so I become entranced with mysteries.
I dream a white haired man leads us to peace.
I do not need a plan just his calm face.
I want not reason, I just want release,
to trace that vision to a safer place.
Then disillusioned I lose all such awe,
knowing the work to make a dream a law.

The process through Northwest Queens

Again and again I asked in pain for salvation,
seeking eternity on Northern Boulevard,
I promised to live only for love.

Any other concern was banished
except maybe how to get my car returned
from the automobile dealership warranty repair shop.

A dakini appeared before me
brandishing a fiery sword.

- could I have the car back by Tuesday?
- no get return by Thursday, you lucky.

I began to wonder if I would ever hear
the lonely sound of a past participle again.

Waiting against hope on Rikers,
the jets in LaGuardia whispered
across the lapsing tide.

New York's Boldest looked at me
with disdain as
coiling all around me,
past razor helical barbed wire,
the families of inmates

shuffled and cursed and pushed
to reach the Q100 bus.

Dante only knew the surface of Hell.
The second level is composed of souls
whose lives conclude neither shame
nor blame, who revolve
through the system endlessly
reincarnating within variations of the same meme
prisoner, guard, visitor, rabbi, lawyer, parole officer,
doctor, coroner, victim.

- I brung my ass all the way down here
only to have this dog sniff my butt, find some weed,
just seed and stems, lucky,
got off with warning, nearly shit myself,
but I aint know that I not been seen my man that day.

on the mudflats near Rikers
a striped bass lays gasping
having known the Antilles,
having swum Northward for decades,
it pointlessly sought to mate
with a can of Ballantine ale.

the fish, who had been previously in the habit of bowing
(προσεκύνουν),
bowed (προσεκύνησαν) even then,
attributing undue hermeneutic significance
to uses of the aorist, an apostate

prostrate before the exegetical fallacy
of this shore.

Mezedes were piled before me,
each an initiation
into deeper Dionysian mysteries,
as I swizzled Retsina
seeking to de-escalate
the ecstasy I felt insurgent
within my breast.

A waitress more beautiful
than any notion I ever had
brought Nescafe frappe
to wash down baklava
and I was transported
to the world of pure ideas.

- where you brought that jacket
sweetheart?

She enticed me
to forsake the ark of my covenant
with Chomsky
that I might wander
upon the shoals of her
immigrant English.

Still I sought,
having long been seeking,

for the way out Van Dam
to the Greenpoint Avenue Bridge,.
I desired perspective
on the conjugations
of time,
when it might not always be now.

As the Chrysler van
ascended up the ramp into the sunlight
all doubts diffused,
and cares were
then allayed.

Disturbing Amherst

she finds alternatives
to rhymes
and disarrays
the metronome of meter
to convey
the infinite
may break through
the infinitesimally mundane.
in our autonomic progress
to the grave
she stops time
casually
as if dusting.
no corner
does she neglect,
nor the beauty
there every moment
as we breathe.
she illuminates
the majesty of daisies
attendant from her
window by the sedge,
in the excitement
in the small
somebodies never
reckon they could need.
to understand

the silence
beneath the elms
in her front yard
she risked obscurity
and perfected
with patient hands
this art
of rearranging words,
each select,
arrayed among the others,
weeds really,
in a temporary vase,
perpetually radiant.

18 ways of looking at a white ball

I.
It feels like it's twenty degrees, the greens
are serrated with frost, the only
moving thing is my eye -
following this white ball.

II.
It was a par three, I greened then
finished the hole after three putts,
no prayer can control this white ball.

III.
The white ball rolled up and hid
within the autumn leaves
like a child playing hide and seek.

IV.
A man and a woman are of one mind,
unless one of them is always thinking
of this white ball.

V.
No one needs to live like this.
I don't know whether
I should loft the white ball with a sand wedge
or I should end it all.

VI.
A trace of snow remains in the bunker.
The shadow of the white ball
stretches across the frozen sand
and the spindrift.

VII.
 No one else is on the front nine;
the sun warms me on the tee;
the white ball rockets from my club
then hits an oak tree
and ricochets and settles behind me.

VIII.
My wife loves me. My children radiate joy.
Yet, here I am this cold October dawn,
cursing after a white ball.

IX.
If I was a skinnier man I would sink more birdies.
Perhaps then people would not walk all over me.
My thoughts are enemies.
There is only the white ball
and the putt in front of me

X.
I know that Chinese sages would sprawl
near this tall white grass
to picnic and drink plum wine.

I have abandoned immortality,
who seek only the white ball.

XI.
When the white ball dribbled
off the fairway
it didn't even frighten the deer.

XII.
If I can't make par on this next hole
then I will disdain the white ball
as incomplete and imperfect
of no use in life
unworthy of my ministrations
and my sacrifice.

XIII.
I followed the white ball as it scurried past the green
there were ledges beyond, levels in hell,
each one of them cost a chip shot.

XIV.
My weight shifts off the back foot and I
turn torque into energy. The white ball
flies majestically in a high arc from this uphill tee.
No king could ever be more pleased
with his dominion.

XV.
The sight of the white ball flying

above orange trees
and yellow trees
and trees insinuating that they too
will fade but are forced to be green yet
confuses me and I lose my ball
and mulligan.

XVI.
The 16th hole rises to a view where you
can see Massachusetts and Connecticut.
Wearing progressive lenses I make out
bare boughs on far away ridges
but I can't find the white ball.

XVII.
 I strike without remorse or repentance.
The white ball moves ceaselessly forwards.
My job is to minimize the stresses it must endure.

XVIII.
It has been the 19th hole all afternoon since that
young lovely in the white skirt
drove by in the refreshment cart.
Somehow we will make the clubhouse
before it starts to snow.
I see a bird land near the
cedar, near the white ball;
it is not a crow, but a blackbird.

Executive Course

Seeking a lost ball, we four probed a hedge.
An arrangement of lilies gave us pause.
We stalled as if confronted by a ledge.
A funeral stench stifled our guffaws.
Fools embroidered on tapestry I saw,
who pranced like medieval innocents,
who facing death were paralyzed with awe.
Startled amid lives festooned with nonsense,
we felt secure that our investment plans
provided endless rounds of distraction,
that years of golf remained in our lifespans.
We let death play through by our inaction,
and grimly realized, deep in the back nine,
shadows hang from a short game in decline.

Nicodemus Mystery

Vengeful jaws
open beneath the world
in which I dwell.

In silence,
insolent of laws,
beneath the artifice which I maintain,
neglected,
curls the craving.

I set the place
as best I can,
aware,
beneath these orderly arrangements,
persists that violent need
much darker than
my soul allows,
more holy than
I care to say.

A ranging beast
lopes after me
though I attend to courtesies,
and would avert
the obvious
if I could beg more time,
that prowls relentlessly,

ready, if I but pause to stare too long,
to pounce through the ordinary
to coil,to strike, to flay all excuses,
to murder all delay.

There is this barking insistence
I drop all pretense
at innocence
or I will be unspeakably defiled
by my obsequious bargain
with the everyday.

There is sharp,
beneath the overt requirement,
the peril, I might have to live,
if I but had courage
to reach beneath these surfaces
to calm the beast that glares at me
as I at him,
to release the urge to flee
what I can't wish away.

Spring in the projects

I am sorry, but
the red brick from this apartment building
is interrupting the honey locust.
I think you were talking.
I can't tell anymore.

Listen to the conversation
among the trees
that has the kids scooting everywhichways
until they eventually become
office workers, carpenters, deliverymen, nurses, rabbis,
thieves.

Wars are waged, fleets set sail.
The calamities of our kind
fail to dismay or waylay them
as they sway
and the rustling leaves
repeat in whispers
the most important things
so they remain remembered.

Venerable ladies, bent double,
congregate by the supermarket entrance.
They know the price of everything.
They may spend the day
palavering, negotiating the river's ebb and flow

but they know
the faint, green light from leaf buds
illuminate the faded brick face
just like this only now.

There are no shortcuts
to paradise; there is no distance at all.
Hidden in plain view
are the remains of all that is beautiful
lost in the fall.

Please take me into the courtyard
and kiss me
for I have lost my place
in this sprawl.

Take me behind the obvious
even if you make me cry.
I trust you to show me
eternity every day.

Hold me so close that
later I will only recall
your hair luminescent
by the retaining wall,
the radiant brick,
and the echoing
of children playing ball.

Garden Party

Between the azalea and I,
never a word was exchanged.
The game between us
was known at a glance.
Secrets can't be left linger between lovers.

I could not let
what I had in mind
get between the peony and me.
We have both wanted one another
and wanted to be free.
We have had too much history.

I bit my lip, retreating.
So beautiful was the phlox,
leaning against the fence,
that I was bereft of all pretense,
open to every advance.
I twisted metaphors all afternoon,
cocktail napkins, in the hands of a shy man,
rehearsing what he wants to say.

I emptied my imagination
before a geranium.
I gave up every preconception
to try to relax and enjoy the plant
implacable before me.

A poem teased me
but every other word
was redacted.
Nothing could be understood.

I knocked at the door of the day lily
and was shown entry into Elysium.
Every moment was intoxicating;
the clocks were thrilled,
and the sun was stopped as it strayed.
Any moment I noticed, dissipated.
Any moment left pass,
offered joy that would not fade.
I was radiant among flowers, as I played croquet.

The seeker

I sought God
but only because I was bored,
trapped indoors one weekend.
It was non-stop rain.
I had run out of things to do.
I had seen every movie before
and there was nothing but weather on TV.

God pounced out at me
as if hiding camouflaged
inside ordinary reality.
I hadn't expected
to be blind-sided.
It was exceedingly unfair in a way
as I had the iPhone in hand at the time
and it could have shattered.

Also, I had nothing in the house
- just limes in the freezer,
a bit of rum, but I had run out of mixer.
Altogether it was a big mistake.
I suppose I invited it
by, you know, "seeking" in the first place.
There is nothing you can do
when this happens
just let it get all numinous, whatever.

In any case, I am not getting excited
ringing doorbells in the neighborhood
jumping up and down and scaring people.
I suppose I will try and be nicer now
that ought to be startling enough.
I will trim my hedges and smile
at passersby.

I will certainly be more careful
in what I ask of people
and of myself
and, you know, God, to try
to avoid mix ups like this
in the future. Sheesh.

Vale puella

"Miser Catulle, desinas ineptire"

Beware the idle class
of idolator you prefer.
They're a little odd
who would nod and defer
while you speak.
You are no god.

All too human
you were in bed,
crueler than any cherubim;
you abetted my disbelief
when my last dream had fled
and rejected me as naive
as I lay naked.

An apostate
from your arms,
I must keep away.
Your sweet words
all thoughts disarray.

Even though you have taken another lover
you must play
and weave together ironies
linking both our names.

I am under no more illusion
that which you pour into my ear
will corrode my brain.
You urge me to ecstasy
You don't care if I am sane.
Your argument is just raw emotion.
You blend together
what I used to pretend
with what I prayed would remain.

If only we had never met
then I would never have known
the kisses I need to forget,
the desire I would forsake
that consumes me, flesh and bone.

I would some other history live
and not struggle to forgive
you for passing off as love
what would end in heartache.

Where you would go I would follow,
once happier than anyone.
On your cheek I've felt the sun
I, who no more believe in light,
regard your smiles but trust none.

I used hang upon the words that passed your lips.
Who bites them now? I must resist

your face more radiant than the apocalypse,
which glares indifferently as I gasp and twist.

I must keep from pouncing onto you,
sheer chaos would ensue.
So I'll steel my heel and turn askew.
Not for a moment were you ever true.
I must obstinately eschew
the beauty that dominates my view
and turn my face into the void
lest wavering I am destroyed.

Marianne

Skulking with the disheveled perverts in first class,
whose fine suits lie soiled
by the unspeakable depravities
of the business day,
on my lap spreads the lurid pink
sheaves of the Financial Times
pitched above this roiling secret.

When you and your sister saunter by,
I am struck like a clock.
You are unspeakably blond,
impossibly tall,
irretrievably plain
and utterly impervious to my gaze.

Forever, I will remember you coiling
to inform your sister
to stop stepping on your heels.
She, but a younger, more vacuous
version of yourself,
all Abercrombie & Fitch,
chewing gum, I could take or leave,
but you, completely pissed off
that you have to be seen
clanking up the aisles with your gangly,
klutzy family, are too much.

I cease fiddling with a memorandum
of understanding that intended
to express, with passion, distress
re: market change
in banking payments,
as you unleash
in your every movement
disinterest for that which is easy.

You, who neither want, nor need,
recreation or sensation,
are as indifferent to phenomena
as any yogini
but entirely more alarming.

As you pass, chaos stirs.
Peace is shattered.
Orderly discussions cease.
Joy leaves those you brush
and hope any you touch.

I don't care that my blackberry
has just fallen to the floor.
I don't care whether my frequent flyer
miles rollover any more.
You fascinate and appall me:
Odi et amo.
Everything about you, your cut socks,

your dangling iPod, the fact that you
don't care that you are flying home to Florida,
your blithe indifference to the prosperity
which has everyday surrounded you,
lures me to your cause.

I don't know why
the airlines are oblivious to algorithms.
You should be able
to get to your seat faster,
rather than be stuck here
bunched behind these yokels
trying to stow luggage.

If only there was an America
worthy of your notice.
If only this country could be original again.

You disdain the conventions
which bind us and find
there is not enough space
in the overhead compartments.
You dismiss the apologies
of the air hostess.
Only a revolution could satisfy you.

Marianne, lead us over the barricades
of our illusions.

Make us realize that all products

and services are poor substitutes
for fun.
Make America young again.
Free us from the tyranny of trends
of tiresome baby boomers.
Agitate your charm bracelet.
Incite this people
to reach for glory
and trample
the mortgaged promise of this country,
sold off as future cash flows.

The infernal symmetries of the everyday
cease to exist in your presence.
You illuminate all delusion.
You resist compromise.

Extreme times, call for your
extremely distant stare.
Steel our spines
that we too might
grow impatient with the obvious.

In just a glance you infuse
the knowledge
that the American hypothesis
is as a mist that blinds us,

the bargains of past generations
are as shopworn
as your jeans.

Liberate us from the inadequate satisfaction
of an exhausted imagination.
Destroy this world,
that a new world be born anew.
Lay waste our preoccupations
and our apologies.
Raze all our frames of reference.

Shatter the arrogance
that imprisons us.
Break through the ignorance
in which we craven cower.
Take torch to the preposterous
banality with which we live our lives.

There is a city
to which we might fly
where everyone is cool
and they dance to techno ragas
besides a swimming pool,
where children delight
in the sunlight
unencumbered by ideologies.

We might unleash movement
locked inside the limits of our desires,

if you would but lead us to that place.
Your refusal to settle
for the necromancy of the past
urges us over the obstacles
that threaten to define us,
that we might arise
as one and storm
the gates of paradise.

Penelope

Retrieving
the string of fictions
she has been weaving
each a moment
that is fleeting,
she insinuates
that she has interest in the entreaties
that dissipate
in the fading light
as she is retreating
resolute and tender voiced
into the dark.

Almost tearful but always polite
Penelope appears distraught
but remains enticing.
She defines limits
that stretch men taut.
She declines
invitations.
She apologies
and later denies
in soothing phrases
her intention
was ever to mislead
those merely mortal to their ruin.

She subdues
those who seek
resolution
of desire.
She deludes men
lured to her
and suspended
as she measures
and maintains
the illusions
that beguile them.

Her house is riot except
that space she commands
immediately around her.
They pursue shadows
who follow her
too closely
having confused
her insinuations with their desire.
She retires in silence
none can touch
as inviolate
as the tomb.

That summer in Ballyferriter

We laughed the whole way home.
It was a little demented;
we were drenched
the minute we started,
and we knew it would take us
over a half hour
shanks mare
up the flanks of Marhin.

The road roared at us.
Water gushed out crevasses.
Our boots were overtopped
and the coats we had clenched
were soon sopping.
The fuchsia were deranged
as we felt along the hedgerows
to deduce the path before us.

If there was music in the world
it was lost that night.
I had to pull at your lapels and yell
full into your face
just to hear myself
above the lashing.

You regarded
my antics with wry detachment

and never even attempted a reply.
You were right to keep quiet
as we slipped
past the leveled monastery.
Flat slabs lay over the clay,
names impressed in lichen,
no one now could read.

The dead in their graves
if they had voices that night
would have upbraided our insolence
Yet, we persisted up the hill,
arms entwined.

I remember touching your cheek
it was so cold.
When we got home,
we fumbled to erect a newspaper tent,
fanning brambles and wet turf,
praying to life each lick of flame
that it might fill the chimney with fire.

After much agony we proved able
and steam rose from our boots
We tended the fire
absorbed with awe
that it could draw moisture
out of the near bog
and then burn it.

Pious before
the votive lamp
we prayed to Jesus
if he would not save
us from the damp.
We turned our faces
towards the eternity
it takes wool socks to dry
innovating from desperation
a way to keep the
trickle that leaked
from them
from wetting
the rest of our clothes.
The window rattled. I got up
to shim frail cardboard in a chink
to keep out the rain.

Clumps of sheep shifted
in the fields out back.
I could not differentiate
them from furze
nor could I tell
where the sky ended
and the world began
for they were all equal
in the squall.

We discussed whether to open the whiskey.

I said we should save it for company.

You made a strong point
that this could be our last night
and you prevailed.
We fell to sleep
side by side in the two armchairs
we had pulled from the parlor.
We had had scarcely a sup
of Powers taken between us.

We were wrenched awake
by sheep bawling
at the indignity of sunlight.
We raced to hang laundry.
After an enormous breakfast
we pulled the armchairs into the driveway.
We could see any car
for miles coming up the valley.
Jackets, cardigans and pants
flapped on the line
happy as magpie
but no happier than you or I.

Graven images

That notion I have
when I close my eyes and pray
might prove more faithful,
than any fantasy.

Worn so its unrecognizable
is this cameo I carry
of your countenance
- You wound me deeper
than I experience.

Yet it is too easy
to evade the obvious,
that which I prefer
and to which I sacrifice
could just be deliberate artifice.

What I force into focus
becomes suffused with grace.
I evoke a misshapen abomination,
a soulless abstraction,
and I bay prostrate before a mask
- afraid, that direct knowledge
maybe obliterates.

Down one long, dark hall, I race.
Memory completes where shadows lapse.

I gulp, my gorge glutted with glossolalia,
articulating praise.

Lashes clinging longingly to the everyday.
I flick butterfly kisses at you,
understanding all preconceptions
are to be deplored;
but cheek to cheek,
in ecstasy, epileptic almost
I drift through trance states.
Flickering in and out of consciousness,
is it any wonder I would have trouble
giving an accurate description to police artists?

The mystery is not solved.
The light's too faint.
Nor is my account reliable.
I identify with those
who bear false witness,
whose testimony is biased.
If only I could be true to you
but I falter. I collapse
bawling before the chalk outline,
a victim too who talked too late.

Seduced by my need for company
I enchain with other lusty devotees
who whip each other
and call out goatishly.

Depraved in their indifference
to ordinary courtesy,
they ignore any difficulty in their ideology.
Convinced through narrow argument
that only they are saved,
they ignore any evidence
that wont fit their narrative
and trample any inquiry.

Have I poured over every crook
in every letter
of every word
in every sentence
in the book,
only to observe you grimace?

I might be mistaken in debating
whether you could be contained,
that some grammar could
convey your meaning.
Each page is strained
and gapes its binding
when shook.

Any who claim this recitation
translate a cascade of motives
whose source is not known;
they net a torrent
never to be tamed.

Perhaps I reason through association,
rather than pause to calculate,
through this fear I share with all men.
We love in name only
afraid to be naked,
unable to see, in the dark.
We trust the fleeting sense of meaning
we give to love,
vulnerable before the incomparable.

I conjure the mystery I need.
Every art is used,
to sustain the spell,
knowing that all too soon
that the only one I fool is me
and I tremble before the void.

I only know I love you more
and more imperfectly each day,
my heart forever vacillates.
Yet, love is perfect, never dismayed,
immanent in all I see.

I might as well appreciate
the mercy I can trace
in the features of the face
radiant before me.
The distance between us
is erased and
I may ford the flow

once I plunge
through the surface tension
between what I need to love
and what I need to know.

A mask

The shaman shows the pain we dare not face.
He sucks poison from those raw wounds we hide
and roots out demons from their resting place.
He brings to light deeds otherwise denied.
The showman shames us into facing pain,
as he slips beneath the smiling rictus
into which we twist too shy to complain.
He speaks aloud what we never express.
Who tries on pain absorbs its slow poison.
To stand for us, to dare under heaven
to take on our struggles and confusion,
to strip apart the memes from which we're spun,
an actor risks his psyche every day
with no more shield than a coarse mask of clay.

Blue Moon

I pulled a mask over the face of the world
and bowed though it was made of clay.
It meant more to me than chaos.
It gave shape to the nameless
It made me want to pray.

I gave voice then to the silence.
and taught the icon what to say
It breathed inviolate mysteries.

Before this vision reason was cowed.
Apostate, naked, unashamed.
I danced within the moonlight
and I was not afraid.

The Cheerio Kid

For T. Frey
http://www.youtube.com/watch?v=zyIU7UCRg-M

Signaling as soon as the ball starts spinning
hand in the air calling the play.
Every fan knows he's a threat.
He becomes a streetlamp.
He dodges, he retreats.
He could go anyway.
He becomes the wall by the temple.
He blocks. He makes like he is about to steal.
He rises from the back court.
He throws shapes.
He backpedals. He educates.
As he moves he becomes the alley full of garbage cans,
backyards full of laundry,
hallways of romance.
Swing sets in the playground
frame his drive.
Eternally glorious as he is running
His sneakers barely brush the court.
The crowd roars. He glides effortlessly forwards.
He remains in memory ready to shoot.
The bleachers echo with triumph, now and always.
forever, he is the pride and hope of our seventh grade.
He gets the ball.

He pumps. He fades.
His head goes one way
but his shot comes out a chaos of probabilities
impossible to anticipate.

Never even hesitate

What induces a salmon to leap?
What lures an eagle to dive?
What leads a boy to leave this life?
We may never know
the indignity or disorder
that caused him, like Ajax,
to drop his shield,
to cease all struggle,
to end all strife.

For now, go through the motions,
mutter the words of your devotions.
Allow yourself to feel deranged.
Write with fire your emotions.
Tell the skies how you have changed.

Attempt, although at first
you will find the effort appalling,
to love this world anew.
Be glad that you have loved him.
Let grief expose you
to those who need consoling.
Love recklessly and without controlling
or limiting your liability to loss.
Love ceaselessly, relentlessly, intimately
the world which brought such suffering to you.
Love each other
and love your son

though you doubt,
you waver,
your thoughts degenerate.

Among calamity and disarray
you will find repeated opportunity
to return to this world the gifts
he gave: faith, hope and charity.

Return to the world
his love, however much you ache,
never pause, never even hesitate.

Pleiades

By wayward grace
returns to me
this cold November night,
the Pleiades.

The indifferent wheel
on which I am pulled
turns whether I delight in science
or succumb to mysteries.

If I have a story
that explains,
can I predict effects?

I might understand the mechanics
of celestial orbit
but cannot pretend
to comprehend the way
this arc intends.

I stretch my arms
as if to frame the infinite.
I can approach
by approximations
but never be intimate.

It is forty years
since I stood beneath
the span at Throgs Neck

and scanned the skies
above the Eastern water.

Disconsolate and arrogant,
impetuous and insouciant,
I regret now that I proved
unable to resist
the riot in the tide
that made my days race
and coarsened my senses.

I wish that I was
more attentive to the landscape.
Luminous souls
strutted about Maritime,
in search of honesty,
and were randomly entangled
in intrigues, loves, rivalries.

For some I only knew the name
to match the face,
for others I only knew their instrument.
I cannot extricate from memory
what distance divided us.
It might have been no more
than wanton circumstance.

Still if I had planned my life,
as I do everything now,
I would have known you,
laughter and trials.

We might have entertained
some other fate
in some universe parallel to this.
Here we disdained
but ritual courtesy.

Still we bent our heads
and bent our elbows too last night.
We peered into each others faces
and spoke quickly our most awful truths.
There were no youth in college dorm rooms
more sincere than we,
for all our indifferent history.
We stopped the senseless
progress of the heavens
and shared a pride
in our predicament.

I may only see you
the odd reunion
but I swear by these beacons
that blaze the winter's skies
we are no more vaguely classmates,
we are friends.

Though the years
have had their way with us
and the wear and tear might be expected
to make us grow complacent,
we remain restless

and as keen to experiment
as when we bet on Purchase in the first place.

We share that fire
stolen from the heavens,
the desire for more
than this world is able to anticipate.

I will eagerly listen to you relate
with amusement
your latest accomplishment
when next we meet
beneath the stars.

The Coast of Victoria

Let the wind strip me of silence
and the rain inanity.
as I scuttle from the crashing din
to escape the sea's depravity.

Is there a God who set me here
to watch me twist as I dodge pain?
Am I supposed to subside in fear,
to cease my climb, to buckle from the strain?

Am I to loose my grip, to raise my hands to pray,
stripped upon these cliffs of all I contain?
Am I meant to bow to this disarray
to prostrate before what I can't explain?

The only purpose that has dignity
amid all this roiling debris
is to live lives without pity
before we relent to the skirling commotion
and slide into the sea.

Not Even Here

Is there, help me, a God who isn't here,
who I am not able to recognize,
who's beyond all I have come to revere,
who is rid this immanent paradise?
There's this grace in all things to which I cleave,
a strained, strange sensation which I insist
informs the core of all that I believe.
What I've perceived may not in fact exist.
I've tried to force the image to cohere,
Yet it disappears faster than I know.
That presence fades I prayed would persevere,
now lost like thunder muffled in the snow,
as all about me each stray, drifting flake
disintegrates in silence and I shake.

Southbound Metro North

Commuters shiver when they sit down.
Clipping my ear I then hear their personalized ring tones.
No one on this train notices
the moment when inertia is overcome.

The sun, just a streak on the horizon,
they plunder pink newspapers for trading strategies
and dissect the Asian markets for auguries,
suburbanites with pressed shirts buttoned.

More earnest are they than any poets,
more driven than jazz musicians,
these magicians, who from thin air
derive streams of cash flows from others' despair.

The stars are no longer required,
dreams have been put away
the ideals of youth reclaimed
by the ironies on this moving train.

Natural impulses, long since subdued,
memories left on the lawns of Mamaroneck,
the anger of an earlier generation
has been placated, soothed and dismissed.

I thought that youth would last forever,
that I would never bargain with the man,
that I would be valiant, that I would stand;
I have settled for a tidy income and a 401k plan.

When I am old I will be kind.
When dying I will give advice.
Until then I will reinvest my dividends
and not think about it twice.

Vanities flash in the window,
the ambitions I had once;
I wanted change every day
and agitated for an end to sorrow.

I demanded charity and decency
and a more noble society.
My wife and child do not know me,
nor I, any past image of myself.

The sun blazes from the East.
The train races through shadow.
The face I raise to greet this day
is not the face I want to meet tomorrow.

The web

Every click I make, each quiz I take
is detected, collected, classified.
Idly browsing, I forget what's at stake.
To each session a scoring is applied.
Each choice gives voice to my character.
Data-driven marketers take delight
in the surreptitious way they capture
my preferences to model me each night.
A spider snares the unaware with jewels,
mere droplets strung upon a silken net.
Innocents are led by lights set for fools,
entertained before they're struck with regret.
No prize is won without paying some toll.
No prize is worth betraying my own soul.

Subways

The subways proclaim the saints.
Graffiti trace out their symbols.
Everybody's supposed to make out somehow how
everyone needs love.

Nothing is explained. The express rushes past.
The garbled address system fails to tell us what we already
know.
Heaven is nowhere if not here.
Service is disrupted.
Help those who suffer.
There will be no other announcements.

The crowd is wowed by the obvious.
The knowledge rattles them to their soles.
They don't have to wait for eternity.
They don't have to go downtown to be cool.
They don't have to wait the trumpet. Judgment is now.

Faint Music

Faint music strains through the gates of heaven,
the sound of clashing wills of working men.
The elect in lofty transcendent spheres
thrill to the grinding of our doubts on fears.
The agitation of thwarted desires
animates the prayerful in their choirs.
Amusing to them are our lusts, our shame,
the lengthy arias from those who blame
their mothers for their twisted circumstance.
Discord revives those lost in timeless trance.
Duets from youth snarled in peccadilloes
delight those chanting eternal rondos.
No harmony can be sustained in life.
We entertain the angels with our strife.

Past it all

I vaguely remember
those arrayed about my bed.
They beam at me uncomprehendingly.
However benign their intent
they fail to sense
the depraved indifference
with which I approach my demise
or their entertainment.

Attempts to comfort
have cloyed,
to be clever, have only annoyed.
All the social conventions
I have strived to avoid
come toppling after me
into the void.

What friendships that survive
lie cracked open,
blistered with ironies.
Figures appear then fade,
no more substantial
than the desire
that used animate me.

I would shoot from one pursuit to the next,
breathless in headlong delusion.

No experience could abate
my insatiable appetite,
no refuge would abet
my ceaseless invagination.
Desires now disintegrate before my eyes.
Beauty that delighted me,
Music that excited me,
Scents that incited me,
Flavor that tightened me,
Touch that ignited me,
Every sensation comes to die
Fears die.
Memories die.
Every one who eulogizes
and remembers me must die.
Soon all will be forgotten,
my passion dust,
that which seeks peace will expire,
the earth itself will disappear in fire.

No delicacies of art or music remain.
I am unable to frame
any explanation or sustain
any appreciation for the past workings of the intellect.
I may have understood more at some point,
but what science I knew has since retreated,
mocked by the accusation
that any attempt at explanation
is absurd besides my inevitable collapse.

No philosophical abstraction provides
more than a moment's satisfaction.
I feel I owe the universe a retraction.
I have deluded myself and others
but this has produced
but transitory distraction.
Neither disappointment nor sullen rage
contain lasting meaning.
I have lived long enough
to stare down such preoccupation.

The intricate fabric of lies
I have weaved into the narrative of myself
gently rises and falls
like the blanket
across my chest,
that warms my nakedness
and helps me rest.

I ask no one to watch,
no one to wait,
no one to pray.
I ask no end to pain.

With each breath I gain
increased disdain for death.
Why expend zeal
on that which I fear
will never seem real.

I warble away
and most of its gibberish
but it comforts those listening
that I am attempting to communicate.
What I am trying to say, I guess
is that I only made progress
at the point of death.

I have worshipped no false gods, at any rate,
kept that one commandment;
let a laugh be my last breath.

Curling

Curling commentators
failed to predict this Olympics.
It's as if all that is decent that's at stake
is in danger of being ignored.

Americans swerve about,
self destructively, angrily.
Canadians with sublime indifference
glide through Riemann functions.

The marks they make in the ice,
transient signatures of their national psyches,
are erased over time by zamboni.

One Bonspiel depends upon
an uneducated and aggravated electorate,
another on comity achieved through comedy.

The Koch Brothers divide America into deciles
to build a farm system they can control.
Canadians are united in horror at the thought.

Stones must loft pass the hog line
with no more force
than to lodge near the button.
Hogged stones must be removed from play.

The skip releases incantations to the ice.
Sweepers attempt to influence trajectory.

Rotating 2 1/2 times,
a stone knocks an opponent's stone
leading it from the house.
With that sound I become aware,
I am unprepared for death,
and I wonder why,
only in moments like this,
I am even alive.

St. Nicholas of Tolentine

St. Nicholas of Tolentine is where I found free love.
Catholic school plaid uniforms appeared as psychedelic
as any mandala in any headshop in Haight Ashbury.
Peaceful, loving people would swarm the heights above
the Major Deegan,
to drink beer and discuss the universe.
Across the river one could see undulating light,
electric arc from the 207th Street Train Yard.
After getting on a buzz,
you could dance in the Knights of Columbus,
North of the Fillmore East, up the Concourse, closer to
the stars.
Then you could make your way to Poe Cottage,
to knock on the door and ask to be let in on the big secret.
Fire trucks would race beneath the EL,
the world would be filled with decibels.
Fights would break out in alleyways.
When high you would learn
phenomena are transitory,
there's no reason to get bent out of shape.
Cops might bust a guy.
His head could be bleeding.
A baby left in his carriage
would cry all night.
A woman, you never knew and would never see again,
would be heaving, sobbing between two parked cars.
All the sadness, all the violence you could ever imagine
was magnified ten thousand fold

behind windows in all directions along the Aqueduct.
All the while beneath the drama,
was the irrefutable groove
that pulled us up from the canvas,
waving smelling salts, yelling get back in the ring,
see beauty everywhere.
By the fire hydrant, one might find a clear spot for off the
point.
Between chalked lines one could hear girls chanting,
playing Hop Scotch.
In the marshes of Spuyten Duyvil, one was could witness
the confluence of tidal waters.
The heart only opens every so often,
like the 207th Street Bridge,
but when and as it does
the Bronx is better than Paradise.

Innocence

I fired the gun.
A second before flight or fight,
I was primed by powdered donuts.
Blame my upbringing
or stresses on my mother's pregnancy.
How I behave is shaped
by circumstances,
epigenetic cascades of proteins,
and eons of predation.
I claim free will out of confirmation bias,
As much the product
of ages of pressure
as turf or coal,
I am unable to unearth the truth,
yet indignant in explaining this story
where I am the hero.
Thank god I have the police union behind me,
because the threat I just faced
was a 12 year old boy.
So I pray,
come what may,
I might sleep at night.

Breathing the same air

Together we are breathing the same air,
saint and sinner, all have, so did Caesar.
The air leaked from souls dying in despair,
the same air infants expel with laughter.
Unseen, except in its effects as wind,
air caresses children playing their games,
it sways trees and stirs old men's memories.
Clothes from laundry lines the wind will exscind.
Vestments, diapers, sail over all our claims,
skimming ships smokestacks, bound for distant seas.
Collapsed civilizations ground to dust,
the minute fibers torn from lives now lost,
are inhaled by lovers bent at their lust.
We breathe again what others did exhaust.

For lost faith

In my prayers
I mention those who have lost faith,
for whom color has been drained from the leaf,
who see frozen earth as barren ground
who find nothing to revere in all that remains,
who confuse vibration in the air for sound,
who gain no glory for all their pains,
those haunted by past belief.

I mention also and bow to those
who cannot see and so do not believe
as if God was some personality
that could be found on Sundays bowling in Great
Barrington.
Science does in many ways deceive.
None of us are entirely fancy free.
We run on a treadmill of perpetual explanation.
Separate yet bound, so we cleave,
and shape ideas of this world as if we had all eternity.
Icons may be abandoned and shunned
not that need deeper than we dare disclose.

I suppose my problem is
God kind of leaps out at me
like an overgrown Labrador puppy.
Whenever I round the corner
there's another encounter.

I struggle to keep balance
to avoid appearing clumsy
but I am after all wobbling
between this world and the next,
feeling giddy.

God is described
as a turkey vulture leaves a tree to fly,
in the geometry of trees against the sky,
in the ache in my side as I enter my fourth mile,
in the fields I race past fallow yet fertile
in the uneven camber of the road,
in the clouds I seek to decode,
in the North wind's intermittent abuse
in the fit of my running shoes,
in a squirrel's improbable caprice,
in the determination of overwintering geese,
in anything I choose
and everything I please
to notice.

A litany of random incidents
are collected as a psalm of praise
to the obvious grace
radiating beneath these surfaces.
In the haphazard and off kilter
I am exposed to beauty
and see nothing more extraordinary
so I sing.

Stylites

Flakes strayed from passing clouds.
The horizon was twisted,
one half purple,
the other pale, yellow.
Exhausted, I had dragged myself to a ridge line.
Aware I could not stop time,
still I wanted to hold the skies, the earth,
and all varieties of religious experience within my mind.
I paused with each heartbeat.
and surrendered to the joy I felt obvious.
Saints in the desert were no better than me on my skis.
The way I saw it we were all in our own ways
whipped into a frenzy of need.
The right combination of contemplative practice
ought trip the lock
so I might enter paradise.
I just knew the glory promised in eternity
was there for the plundering,
if I could work the combinations right.
Anyhow you know how it goes sometimes,
it's all a surprise,
but the grasping, seedy way I leaned into the scene
caught me off balance,
so I tumbled into realizing
how sleazy I was being.
Unlike, say the Desert Fathers who might have earned the
privilege,

I was trying to jack my way into heaven.
Instead of mortifying myself on a pillar exposed to the
sun,
I sported performance base layers.
It might be -15, I would never know.
My arms splayed, poles hanging from my gloves,
I was more an advertisement for sacrifice
than the actual deal,
but pretending made me feel real.
When the light changed again
I caught the number.
Maybe it was my uneven stance,
the continuous incremental strain
beneath the hypervigilance
I would not acknowledge
let alone try to explain,
but as I stood there in the cold,
I slipped into a light trance.
Hills in the distance began to glow red.
The wind subdued.
The last clouds had fled.
I noticed I had been slightly aware the whole while,
as if a frame that was skewed
was nudged a tad,
so that grace ensued,
when I relaxed denial.

The cyclists

Leaning into the effort, they still strive,
rising in their saddles, straining their thighs,
gaining speed against head winds with each drive,
they rally for the contest not the prize.
They excite our memories with their lives,
those cyclists who were slaughtered in sunlight.
No random act of violence deprives
them glory, nor can it spoil our delight
in the struggle to attain excellence.
They raced against the clock as in time trial.
Forever lifted forwards in suspense,
radiating joy throughout that last mile,
never reaching the goal they still desire,
through all eternity they still aspire.

Smart Phone

80 times a day I turn to you, O Phone,
not for information but for wisdom,
to find out all that yet is known
from astrophysics to Islam.
I free associate Wikipedia pages
and study the nicknames of the sages.
With movements more random than Merce Cunningham,
I circumambulate my way through chaos
and with a thousand point connections
contain the world within a word cloud.
I know where now is displayed the Enola Gay
and that Tarquinius Superbus was proud.
When North Korea and the US disagree,
within the limits of the time allowed,
I'll explain to all their history,
and then the chemistry of Turin's shroud.
I know the news before it's shown,
having hacked a passing drone.
I win poker chips by doubling down,
after rating every restaurant in town.
One day I will walk into traffic distracted,
and the internet will be by one subtracted.
Pray for me when I have passed away,
and keep my home page from decay.
Weep not for me or for posterity,
but for the web's integrity

Grand Central

I bow entering Grand Central Station
who have only ever wanted love
to find people waiting in the vestibule
to hug late arrivals.

Tourists radiate peace
as they flash V for Victory
behind selfie sticks.

Businessmen abandon
all pretense of self-importance
as they dance intricately without colliding.

I am confused by the beauty
of ordinary commuters.
Light from the vaulted ceiling proves
they are actually angels.

I concelebrate
as we wheel about the Kaaba
that is the information booth
where true hearts rendez-vous.

Human motivations are elevated
before the tabernacle of the MTA,
that the dust from Manhattan
be lifted from us,
and we purified
who are anointed
with beers to go
as we ride
the last cars to Westchester.

Exiting the Yeshiva

If I only did what was best for me
I would stay in ecstasy.
Short circuited by the idea of God,
I'd transform the earth I trod.
Every contact would energize.
On every side grace would rise.
With peaceful souls I would abide
and all my longing would be satisfied.
But, I must this world negotiate,
ugly mobs consumed with hate,
provocateurs pretending sincerity
charlatans exploiting charity,
pundits extemporizing to deceive
and saints who thrive on what they thieve.
Weary eyes dart back when I smile,
those who trust not after trial,
who detect the whiff of sanctimony
as an attempt to steal their money.
So I too laugh and swear and cry
with all who are born and who must die.
I drink. I fight. I swerve and dance,
intoxicated by this dangerous romance.
I could be wise, I could stay in shul,
or love this world like a crazy fool.

My education

I toss each night through sheets aflame with pain
and wake to find ceaseless hell in daylight.
Flayed almost, so little flesh does remain
mothers must shield their children from my sight.
Might I find salvation in my disgrace?
Is there purpose hidden in suffering?
Ought I perceive disdain as welcome grace?
Is this relentless torture redeeming?
Unendurable agony helps me
connect with those who also know sorrow.
I'm educated by poison ivy;
there's no relief today, none tomorrow.
Each boil's a careful tutor to my soul;
nothing can save me, nothing can console.

Thunderclap

We'd argued. We'd kissed. We didn't want the rain.
The first drops surprised us in the open.
We dashed hand in hand stumbling down the lane,
suddenly again whom we had once been.
Foliage turned preternatural green.
The air became electric with tension.
The ruts we'd run, we could see as routine,
they confined us to lives void of passion.
Exposed, as lightning ripped apart the skies,
alert at once to the phenomenon,
that which we had clung onto as disguise
slipped before the coming cataclysm.
Fall down the rain, rattle the trees above,
that each thunderclap summon us to love.

The canopy of leaves

Unto the canopy I raise my voice.
Leaves radiate with joy I can't explain,
Nothing here has been arranged by my choice.
Each detail seems designed to entertain,
a network of limbs swaying as I sing
light rain accompanying the rapture.
When bowers burst into bloom in the Spring,
blossoms explode with fragrance from moisture.
Boughs groan anticipating the pleasure
of the slowly approaching thunder storm.
Uplifted by gusts, heavy with vapor,
the last thing I notice is the leaves swarm.
Any separate notion disappears.
A curtain's pulled back as the downpour nears.

At sea

The stars offer light
for you, but not for me.
I strive to steer the vessel
of our wrecked matrimony.
You remain polite
scanning distant skies.
Words you know
but will not say,
are left to drift away.
I try reading turgid water
to judge insurgent tides.
Scrawled across the surface,
between roiling waves,
our future's there to scrutinize.
We cannot find safe harbor,
we must save our daughter,
so we ride out the night.
We, two practiced sailors,
who will tighten ropes
and trim the aft sail,
we will do what's right.

Across the river

The breeze blows in from Brooklyn
and here on the Lower East side I inhale
every secret muttered under breath,
love confessed and loved regret,
the sighs uttered in hallways,
the smoke from every furtive cigarette.
Fantasies and insights
coil across the river.
Whispers and reveries tumble through coffee shops.
Unsubstantiated beliefs spill out backyard lots.
Incantations scramble across steeple tops.
I am buffeted by the despair in ripped up betting slips.
Across the shoreline dreamers unfurl their stories,
striking flags that catch the wind.
Ferries repeat their doubts and boasts.
They amplify the needs of the less confident.
Mothers call and no one answers.
It's as if the whole borough is playing ball
and no one notices until hopes begin to waver.
Floating across Wallabout Bay
come heartache and neglect,
deferred passion and abrupt compromise.
I breathe in someone's last breath,
a baby's first gasp, a bishop's laugh.

The smell of fresh laundry
races through the clotheslines
I can just about make out when I squint

down the avenues that reach back
from the waterfront past Bed Stuy
the mysteries of Crown Heights, Brownsville and
Canarsie.

Hart Island

One million dead, penniless,
stacked in trenches, forgotten,
lie on the approach path to LaGuardia.
They could not pay the boatman
and here stranded remain
for all eternity.
They regard passing businessmen,
such as I,
with unblinking disdain.
Dividends could end,
finery be rent,
those proud in flight
might die in penury.
The wine in First Class
on American Airlines
cannot soothe me
nor my usual town car driver
console me when I arrive.
All I know must die.
Which reminds me
someday to swim
from the Bronx
to Great Neck,
to alight, midpoint,
at Hart Island
to give thanks
that I have ever been alive.

The everlasting

We wish them well
who have gone before.
Wherever they now dwell
they need not heed us anymore.

Passing through a veil,
entering the light,
we hope that those we have known die
might find some further life.

Whispering in the breeze
repeated memories
drift but cannot stay.

We mistake what shapes we may
as we struggle each succeeding day
longing those who've passed away.

Unable to confront despair,
some take old clothing from the dead
and drape these on an empty chair
to halt the pain they can't control
to call back that departed soul.
We dread what we will find ahead.
We implore those beyond all care,
then hear what each of us believes,
a voice or rustling in the eaves.

We're limited in imagination
stunted, confused, distracted by shadows.
What we expect is shaped by past sensation,
as fleeting as the order we'd impose.
We use belief to explain sacrifice,
filling the void with all we've ever known,
thinking eternity is this world twice,
completing such pattern as we are prone.
We force our follies into a story
to justify daily indignity,
confusing chaos and allegory
starved all our lives for meaning and beauty.
How accurate could be our forecasting?
Nothing we have known is everlasting.

Resistance

Mimic the keys that lock each cell,
insinuate your tropes into the story
that forms my soul,
I feel you, virus, as you repeat cliche.
I hate that you rhyme molecularly
and despise your nattering anaphora.
Try as you will to steal my breath
I exhort hematopoietic armies
to swarm within my bones,
to sharpen and hone lymphocytes
against the antagonism in my blood.
Let them scorn those trite phrases
I would utter only when not myself
and attack and rally and attack
until these foes are shredded into alphabet.
Within each affected cell,
let cannons in intrinsic response roar,
and shower the invader with proteins hot as steel.
While I, above the battlefield, meditate,
as my diaphragm rises and falls,
adrenaline increases
and every fiber of my being rouses to retaliate.

Pangur Ban

My cat and I,
we pray each day
I have doubts,
and he has fleas.

Our prayer sails
through time and space.
Beneath these stars where my faith fails
He grooms his paws with guileless grace.

I visualize in minute detail
trials of saints in the face of hell.
My cat when he's not swatting at his tail,
crouches and feints
stalking prey only he can smell.

I spend hours translating verse
simplifying so that laymen can understand.
He with equal fervor will immerse
his will in shredding yarn, separating every strand.

Each of us masters a separate skill,
I, words, he, the kill.
Neither stays while the other labors
as individual as any neighbors,
who take delight when the other scores,
we quiet destinies fulfill
enjoying triumphs the wider world ignores.

Grace

I race headlong towards the open grave
leaning forward as I pound the terrain.
Resolute pursuing the goal I crave,
fixed on the distance, disdaining each pain.
Salvation awaits if I can proceed
without wavering, threading narrow straits,
straddling hurdles, not slackening speed,
though with each step my frame reverberates.
I chance on a rat splattered on the road
who scarpered seeking some promised reward,
and I am disturbed by this episode.
There's a beauty here that can't be ignored.
Eternity's not some faraway place,
even the flattened rat radiates grace.

Manfred

I cried within the immutable frame
in which I'd been ensnared - where I served time.
No one could hear me. Bound, I wept for shame.
Trapped within the existing paradigm,
I stumbled irretrievable pathways,
hemmed on all sides by cognitive bias.
I turned the same way always through the maze,
boxed-in, as if by the Himalayas,
kept from conceiving any dimension,
I was unable to visualize.
Blinded, as if I'd stared into the sun,
I'd squat confused and mocked by my own cries,
the prisoner of my own narrative
which I'd escape if I'd myself forgive.

Our Chemistry

Polymers were combined in solution,
information expressed chemically,
these mutated to become you and I.

As the result of long evolution
pleasure and pain entangle ceaselessly
- serotonin's released each time we cry.

Harming you was never my intention.
I seem to crave stress intermittently,
My impulsive reactions run awry.

Songs come to life after hard truths are won.
Relief follows enduring agony.
Endorphins flow from hurtful stimuli.

We're not limited by our chemistry
Let's love now and transform eternity.

Along the road to Damascus

Diaphanous strands of polyester
are presented to us as angel hair.
Trees are hewn for one we had to murder,
the one who asked us love more than we dare.
Strings of electric lights and chintz recall
the hope that came to us one cold, dark night.
Depraved, we seek escape and each day fall.
We go through hell to love less than we might.
The gifts we care to stack near the manager
are mere tokens of what is really asked,
to love always regardless of danger,
to assist the stranger and the outcast.
Go find and shelter those the world abhors.
Share mercy with those fleeing distant wars.

Temptation

The devil in the desert dared Jesus
to turn away from this world in despair.
He derided compassion as specious,
acts of charity as pointless as prayer.
The father of lies declaimed we're naive,
deluded by dreams disjoint from meaning.
Death, he hissed, undermines all we believe.
We chase conceits then die. Life's demeaning.
Stop your senses. Relax from care. Exhale.
Meditate on endless expanding joy.
Surrender to oblivion. Inhale.
Use such tricks as you're able to deploy.
The Lord replied, this world was made to love
If you can't find peace here, you won't above.

Sunday mornings

Across this city, church steeples would ring.
Low tones would reverberate from afar.
Echoes would influence my wandering.
Maybe, I'd spy you leaving a wine bar.
Thinking I might have heard nearby your heels,
I would be drawn reluctantly downtown
to probe what each distinct corner conceals.
Sunday dawn, roaming streets of past renown,
I'd forget that time with you meant torture.
Clanging would recall me to that torment.
Delusions might fade, heartache would endure.
Where I searched, I found just empty pavement.
Years that have passed have failed to dull the pain.
Bells would stop, were you in my arms again.

Orion

Orion, wow, you're way on the right already,
One AM! I thought I was paying attention,
Winter is just sailing by.
I need to hold myself steady
before I start to sway.
I am in this weakened state
open to suggestion
as to whether the geese pool,
beyond the copse of birch
or among the straw
by the irrigation ditch.
I hear them call
but can't tell which
I'd rather believe
the evidence of the senses
or my dreams.

Tashlikh

I long to lunge into the harbor
to run and jump from an empty pier
to plunge lustfully into the cold waters
as if sea nymphs called to me,
and I was freed of the claims
of this earth's daughters.

I would dive beneath the surface
and for some time disappear.
I would hear only the surge
of my own heart in my ear.

Freed of the need to replay
the insinuations, the recriminations,
the long drawn conversations,
that I have come to fear
I would sport and play.

Onlookers could doubt my sanity
but as I'd break through the waves
I would arch my back to mock
those who cling to safety.

As I slipped past the mooring chains
that drag beneath the stanchions
I would pull away
from all that I have craved.

I would forget how lethargy once gripped me,
how I was indifferent, and depraved.
I would make my way to the open ocean
with every stroke I would become stronger.

I would exhaust myself of emotion
and I would taste the salt spray.
The insurgency in my breast
would be transmuted.
I would be lulled by the motion
within the breakers.
I would roll and sway.

No regret would detain me,
self doubt would not weigh on me,
nor guilt again waylay me,
I would never fear that I might drown.

Let me pack the bread I brought
to cast to the gulls
and return from staring out to sea.
I thought I might escape pain,
let me make my apology.

I reject now all that dulls.
I would encounter all
that is difficult
to restore all that is my fault
to soothe you

whom I have treated with disdain.
As I face the source of all past failure,
let me first forgive myself,
that I might your love secure.
Let us entwine one to another
more tightly than before
to make a knot that cannot fray.
For without you I will drift
and I will be washed away.

Beyond the shore

Beyond the shore,
where mermaids sing
in language unrelenting,
poets seduced by rhythms
they fail to comprehend,
flailing keep on pretending until they drown.
The impudent attempt to stretch assonance across the
ocean
is shredded by gales
which whip the surface of the obvious.
None dare describe the awful silence in the tide
that breaks upon these rocky shoals
conceits rashly constructed, too frail to survive.
Metaphors twist into meaningless shapes.
Allegories drift like shattered hulks
whose stanza list before they sink into oblivion.
Scattered vowels are snatched away by gulls
gluttonous for any morsel.
Bobbing consonants succumb to waves
whose motions never cease.
Nothing but flotsam remains
of the original idea.
Entropy overcomes all artifice.
Words cannot convey
the intricacies of the need
floating debris communicates.

The psalm is not the song as sung nor its intention
but is apiece with that virtue we have won
who swim beyond the summons to concede
to the cruelty of the sea.

Daylight beautiful again

Lord, I am sure you want me
to drop to my knees
to magnify your name,
but I was celebrating creation all last night,
singing without cessation.
So I am now a tad dehydrated.
Lift from me this hangover
so I am no longer thirsty.
Illumine me so I am no longer confused
by that which is transitory.
Make plain the way to eternity,
that I glory in the everyday.
Spare me thy iniquity,
I am on uneven ground.
Stop this world from spinning,
I could use respite from suffering,
as I learn nothing from pain.
Take me outside time.
Let it already be tomorrow
that I have drunk plenty of fluids,
and find daylight beautiful again.

Last Business

Nausea, acrophobia, doubt
whorl through the atrium.
The glass floor shatters
in this elevator.
I want to believe
as I lunge through space
if I can hold the pose
I might gain enough momentum
to clear the lobby.

If I have enough will
to clasp the vines that spill
from each balcony landing,
there is a way to stop me falling.

I have to survive this business.
as I hurtle toward the wall
I hear whispers through the roaring chorus
each voice, a different opinion, calling.

I am, no one in particular,
a story, contradicted by witnesses,
a difference, without distinction,
the product of a divided conscience,
the random result of autocatalytic process,
a meaningless fluctuation in a field of chaos,
here in the last moments I have to live

I can't even compose a compelling narrative
I have what? Forty years until I smash the pavement?

I am lost in the lobby of a Marriott
unable to strip the last illusion
from myself
to experience fully
the hospitality here on offer
to decrypt the semiotics
of the hotel staff
to deconstruct their frailties
and rejoice in our common humanity
only desire gets in my way
I need to check my luggage
to retrieve it later
and I can't seem to get
anyone's attention
not even my own.
I am busy rewriting meeting minutes,
assigning next steps with due dates
to customers whose motives
I have modeled as Markov chains,
eliminating the points of resistance to the sales pitch,
maximizing opportunities, neutralizing threats,
identifying the unit costs, benefits and success criteria
needed to build the business case,
wondering if I might catch an earlier flight,
will I get upgraded.

I glance at the blackberry

that tells me I am missing
much more than a conference call.
I am missing the chance
to be nice to people.
So, I smile
and they don't even see
me
crash.

Gentians

Among mountain wastes I struggle. My gait
stumbles, high at altitude, blasted by light.
With each exertion I try to extirpate
the humiliation of my cursed plight.
If there is a promise that's here innate
in these rocks and crags I'll claim it my birthright.
It's worth risking rearrangement of my spine,
to reach past what's human to grasp the divine.

Hypoxic in a hypnotic trance, I
urge every muscle with each strained breath to work,
to transcend, to defeat what I deny
that I'm but flesh, a fluke, a random quirk,
a bit of frolic, and that in a flash I'll die.
I clamber against this fate. I go berserk.
Mere reason's sacrificed upon the altar
as ritually I climb and falter.

Peering back at me from within the ice
there is a corpse frozen, fast in mid-exploit.
This wayward pilgrim has paid too high a price.
barricaded in rime, no more adroit
now than the gutted, pitted, weathered gneiss
that caresses him however maladroit
and fixes him in rapture as in life
with a look as hard and cold as any knife.

It's clear to see how much he must have fought.
He tried not to succumb to slumber or ease
but rests in death. I'll beware every thought,
keep vigilant, though eyelids blinking crease.
Though exhausted, I will remain distraught.
Though hallucinations lure, I'll trust no peace.
This mind might help illuminate the way
if only held but lightly as I sway.

No natural fear can I hold, no kind
of obsession, for all that I survey
will consume attention, lead astray my soul.
I can't hate what history has consigned
to me though so inclined. I can't cast away
any particle of pain for the whole.
Nor can I care that some part of me survive.
I do not care I suffer, just that I strive

A kind word might close the gap between us;
- one still groaning salutes one frozen still.
All feeling's drained from limbs, we're beyond fuss.
Each of us, it transpires, lacks the will to will.
Each glares in silence ready to discuss
and argue the purpose struggle's meant to fill.
Both resigned to glory in this sporting life,
we mock the same dream and share this same strife.

We've lifted up our lives in sacrifice
to transubstantiate our pain and loss.
Separated by desire from paradise,

we were lured into these wild wastes to cross
the distance that divides us. Across the ice
we stare one breathless and one about to gloss
all distinction at the event horizon
merging into what's wanted from the mountain.

Deus intimior intimo meo.
God's closer to me than I am to myself
I remember now what I learned long ago
More is related to me on this shelf
on the precipice of now than I can know.
This peak I'll summit if I deny myself
the need to limit or define the climb
to belittle myself before the sublime.

Indifference strikes me as the easy way
to maintain the fiction that I am free
to ignore that chaos erodes each day
my every plan, and yawn as dignity
is lampooned by fortune, that I a toy of clay
could form any image of the deity.
However amused I am to be alive
I should shrug off each fancy I contrive.

God intimidates me more intimately
than I intimate to myself. The fear
is there if I but stare at things minutely.
Nothing has ever prepared me to be here.
I know that all I pretend is not me,
and know that reckoning I dread draws near.

Any moment I might realize my flaws
are pointless and my existence without cause.

There is no intimacy I could take
that God's not already taken with me.
I hide from discovery. I start to quake
yet not with fear. I do not want to flee
but persevere in awe though my limbs shake
as all I see arcs towards eternity.
There's tension fraught beneath the frozen stone
more immediate than any urge I own.

Mere intimations suggest, tease, enthrall.
I lust for veils afraid of what I'd bare.
Interfering with this unmentionable
fear of self disclosure is a self aware
that all selves are motions for dismissal.
Shorn of all vestiges, exposed to the air,
I'm stripped of all save love on this arete
no higher can I aspire not in Tibet.

There is nothing I've had to do to prepare.
Nothing esoteric I had to hone
No effort was required, I always was aware.
Love is all I've needed; the love I've been shown.
All else is empty, whipped into the air.
I stagger downhill now chilled to the bone.
The only love is in the world I know
among people, not in this drifting snow.

In the small I might find my salvation
by giving all I have in every act
insisting on love, without hesitation,
intent on detail, particular, exact
trying just to help without cessation
paying quietly in deeds for all words lacked
There's nothing more between us and the distance
to God than this gift I bring, these gentians.

The end of the world

Drain-spouts jut into alleyways gushing rain.
Wave follows wave in the gale.
There is nothing you can believe with your eyes.
All buildings look like home.
Every door appears the same.

Umbrellas can't stave off salvation.
Grace comes pelting
the heads of the unprepared
and the prudent,
irrespective of their plans.
If our hearts are not irrigated,
God has been trying to inundate us,
we have only ourselves to blame.

Automobiles, with windshield washers
switching everywhichways,
ease forwards,
drivers peering after road signs
invisible in the slanting melee.
They are not lost.
That which they seek
remains with them always.

Commerce is halted.
The awnings of each business
are way stops
for commuters scurrying to stay dry.

No one is buying
what is on sale anymore.
Commodities do not constitute relations.
We make our own sunshine.
We are content with each other
or damned forever
to mope and malign.

The pavement is slick underfoot.
There is no point in running,
no way to dodge the obvious
Why continue denying?
We have been in paradise
the whole while.

Each face is a gateway.
Each trial is the secret passage.
This storm is the opportunity of our lives.
No one is in anyway different.
All arbitrary distinctions are washed away.
If we can't come together now,
there might not be another day.

The process to poetry

Graceful cascades of consonants
alliteratively eliding between sentences,
a rivulet rippling over rock face
flitters between analogy and naked need.

A glorious effusion of vowels
reverberate within an open shell.
The distant ocean roars its disavowal.
I confuse the hypoxia from sudden beauty
with mystical experience.

Through mentalese a voice leads me.
I am aphasic, able to repeat but rhythms.
Prostrate I crawl on my hands and knees
trying to find through melodic intonation
the intention I hear only as phrasing.

I repeat back the tempo in rhyme.
Forgive me, o muse, most human angel,
I feel compelled to keep time.
While on this earth I dwell,
I eke mortal compromise
in the silence between each syllable.

Between jubilation and requiem,
I deduce the syllabus
by sounding out
the secrets enticed from me

whose meaning remains
layered beneath my breathing
more mysterious than any psalm
this mortal could devise
as holy as the love
which you and I continues to contrive.

Europa

Divine, despite entering mortal guise,
a god might come to experience pain
but never that gushing fear, this surprise
might be the last thrill ever on this plane.
Zeus regards the loss of love with a sneer.
He repeatedly re-enacts his lust.
Mechanically he will persevere
used to subduing his lover's disgust.
Outside of time yet compelled to rhythm,
he is roused contretemps in the meadow
to consummate nature's most sacred hymn.
He thinks he sings but she hears him bellow.
Broad of face and heart, Europa endures
gods, men, their narratives and overtures.

Composure

One dare not stare too long into the sun.
The glory of God is also blinding.
Regard them both with averted vision
noticing without completely minding.
Ecstasy threatens about the garden
as we're surrounded by the beautiful.
The slightest breeze commands my attention
to harken this world's blatant miracle.
Bees buzz the glade. Birds sing out entreaties.
Flowers bud then bloom throughout the afternoon.
Countless joys require all my expertise,
I must maintain composure as I prune.
These shears I wield cause much fragrance to flow.
Every corner yields fresh cut willow.

Our arrangement

You play a melody upon my hips
lightly with your fingertips.
Devastated, by the improvisation,
I lose all will
and all sensation.

Slinking to the pillow,
I am unable to resist the obbligato,
expecting that you will not tease
nor mislead me with leitmotif.

I prop myself up
but I never anticipate
your next movement.
Your left hand dissuades
me from ever wanting to leave you,
your right makes me disintegrate.

This afternoon is more depraved
for the insinuation you sustain
that between us thrives illicit tension
I quaver past caring
if this will end in resolution.

The suspense drives me insane;
it's the strain of trying to please
someone who alternatively
excites and ignores me,

who withdraws
but won't leave me.

I hear the glissando
whenever you near me,
but realize too late you are just keying me
for some new arrangement.

Your opening theme
is never sincere.
You declare intention, only to lead
me through variations.
You might kiss me alright,
but you don't want love
you want counterpoint.

Tip of the tongue

Each blow's awful in the long, slow onslaught.
Monuments collapse. Stone walls turn to clay.
Constant cannonade reduce all to naught
as memory and intellect decay.
Your reasoned arguments trail into space.
The words you require evade your recall.
You refuse retreat though you lose your place.
Frustrated, you grow angry as you stall.
Letheologica threatens our friendship.
Time erodes our decades' long colloquy.
Though now I always beat you to the quip,
I take no joy in Pyrrhic victory.
Expect no quarter old adversary,
with deft care I'll defend the contrary.

The Mouse

More pernicious than the Hantavirus
that vermin spread from mouth to filthy paw,
is a threat more likely to destroy us.
Spread too by a mouse, it causes slack jaw.
Predictable routines and slapstick schemes
repeat to lull and slowly mesmerize
to produce children docile to his memes,
audiences primed to commercialize.
Let children restlessly experiment,
push, pull, tussle and grapple, prod and poke.
They should roar and explore, never relent,
bursting prior confines, so grows the oak.
Beware setting children before TV.
Let no mouse contain creativity.

The May Fly

God loves, no less than any one of us,
the May Fly, who knows the briefest glory,
who surveys aloft this earths detritus
with perspective after one days folly,
who attempted once aerial ballet
and was buffeted by adversity,
who sought a mate with this brazen display
to prove his dauntless productivity.
You who dare to pray to live one more day,
dust motes don't float for long in a sun beam,
moments squandered wont come again your way,
bask in the headwinds or drift in a dream.
Eternity is what you make it, son.
Use what light's left before this evening's done.

The Latch to the Garden

Time disappears. All thoughts and cares take flight
when the latch to the garden is lifted.
Teeming leaf glow translucent in sunlight.
Ordinary perspective is shifted.
Wildflowers pulsate chaotically
as they are stroked by swarms of butterflies.
Displaying their bold colors wantonly,
they thrive by using blossoms as disguise.
No matter we're apart I am content.
Having loved you with my entirety,
I have no reason ever to lament.
Attending you, I'm quick to find beauty.
Stamen quivering, laden with pollen,
being touched, thrill it might happen again.

www.ingramcontent.com/pod-product-compliance
Lightning Source LLC
Chambersburg PA
CBHW061829040426
42447CB00012B/2888